HOW TO USE CALL RECORDING AND TRANSCRIPTION IN IOS 18.1

A Comprehensive Guide to Enhancing Communication and Productivity on Your iPhone 15 Pro and Pro Max

RAY JOE

Copyright © by Ray Joe 2024. All rights reserved.

Before this document is duplicated or reproduced in any manner, the publisher's consent must be gained. Therefore, the contents within can neither be stored electronically, transferred, nor kept in a database. Neither in Part nor full can the document be copied, scanned, faxed, or retained without approval from the publisher or creator.

Table Of Contents

INTRODUCTION

CHAPTER ONE

CHAPTER TWO

CHAPTER THREE

CHAPTER FOUR

CONCLUSION

Introduction

Overview of Call Recording and Transcription Features

With the release of iOS 18.1, Apple has introduced a significant enhancement to its iPhone functionality: the ability to record and transcribe phone calls. This feature is currently available on the iPhone 15 Pro and iPhone 15 Pro Max models running the iOS 18.1 developer beta. Users can initiate call recording during a conversation by tapping a dedicated icon, which also triggers an audio notification to inform all participants that the call is being recorded. The recorded audio, along with its transcription, is automatically saved in the Apple Notes app, allowing users to easily review important conversations later.

Importance of Call Recording and Transcription

The integration of call recording and transcription serves multiple purposes, particularly in enhancing communication and documentation. For professionals, this feature is invaluable for capturing details from meetings, interviews, and important conversations, ensuring that critical information is not lost. The transcription provides a text record that can be searched and referenced, making it easier to find specific information without having to replay the entire audio. Additionally, the automated nature of the transcription process allows for efficient documentation without requiring manual note-taking, thereby improving productivity and accuracy in various settings, from business to personal use.

Furthermore, the legal compliance aspect is addressed through the automated notification that informs all parties about the recording, fostering transparency and adherence to privacy laws. This feature not only enhances user experience but also aligns with Apple's commitment to privacy and user rights.

CHAPTER ONE

Getting Started

Requirements for Using Call Recording and Transcription

To utilize the call recording and transcription features in iOS 18.1, users must meet specific requirements:

Device Compatibility: The feature is exclusively available on the iPhone 15 Pro and iPhone 15 Pro Max models. These devices are equipped with the necessary hardware and software capabilities to support the advanced functionalities of Apple Intelligence, which powers the transcription process.

Operating System: Users must have the iOS 18.1 developer beta installed. This version includes the newly introduced call recording and transcription features, which were not part of earlier beta releases or the initial public version of iOS 18.

Installing iOS 18.1 Developer Beta

To install the iOS 18.1 developer beta, follow these steps:

Enroll in the Apple Developer Program: Users must be registered as a developer or part of Apple's Beta Software Program. This enrollment provides access to beta versions of iOS.

Backup Your Device: Before installing any beta software, it is advisable to back up your iPhone to prevent data loss in case of any issues during installation.

Download the Beta Profile: Visit the Apple Developer website or the Beta

Software Program page to download the beta profile.

Install the Profile: Go to Settings > General > Profile on your iPhone and install the downloaded profile.

Update Your Device: After installing the profile, check for the iOS 18.1 update in Settings > General > Software Update and follow the prompts to install it.

Supported Devices

The call recording and transcription features in iOS 18.1 are supported on the following devices:

- iPhone 15 Pro
- iPhone 15 Pro Max

These models are specifically designed to leverage the new AI capabilities introduced in iOS 18.1. Other iPhone models, including the standard iPhone 15 and older devices, do not support these features due to hardware limitations.

How to Record a Call

Step-by-Step Instructions for Recording

To record a call on your iPhone running iOS 18.1, follow these steps:

Initiate a Call: Open the Phone app and make a call as you normally would.

Locate the Recording Icon: During the call, look for the recording icon, which resembles a waveform and a circle, located at the top left corner of the screen.

Start Recording: Tap the recording icon. You will hear an audio alert stating, "This call will be recorded," notifying all participants that the recording has begun.

End the Recording: To stop recording, tap the recording icon again. You will receive another audio notification indicating that the recording has ended.

Access Your Recording: After the call, the recording and its transcription will be saved in the Apple Notes app, where you can easily access and review them later.

Understanding the Recording Icon

The recording icon is crucial for initiating and managing the recording process. It appears as a small waveform symbol combined with a circle, indicating that the feature is active. When you tap this icon, it triggers the recording function and simultaneously alerts all call participants about the recording. This transparency is designed to comply with legal requirements regarding call recording.

Notifications During Recording

Throughout the recording process, there are several notifications:

Initial Notification: When you start the recording, an audio message informs all participants that the call is being recorded. This is a critical feature to ensure everyone is aware of the recording.

Ongoing Notification: While the call is being recorded, a timer will display on the screen, showing the duration of the recording.

Ending Notification: When you stop the recording, another audio notification plays, indicating that the recording has concluded. This ensures that all participants are aware that the recording is no longer active.

These notifications help maintain transparency and legal compliance during conversations.

CHAPTER TWO

Accessing Your Recordings

Locating Recordings in Apple Notes

After recording a call on your iPhone with iOS 18.1, you can easily locate the recordings in the Notes app. Here's how to access them:

Open the Notes App: Launch the Notes app on your iPhone.

Find the Call Recordings Section: At the top of the app, you will see a dedicated section labeled "Call Recordings." Tap on this section to view all your recorded calls.

Select a Recording: From the list of recordings, tap on the specific call recording you wish to access. This will open the recording along with its transcription.

Understanding the Call Recording Note Format

The format of the call recording notes in the Notes app is designed for clarity and ease of use. Each recording is labeled with the date and time of the call, making it straightforward to identify when each conversation took place.

Transcription Layout: The transcription of the call is organized into paragraphs, clearly indicating who is speaking at various points in the conversation. This helps users follow along and understand the dialogue more easily.

Summary Feature: At the top of the transcript, there is a Summary button. Tapping this will generate a concise overview of the call, highlighting the main points discussed. This feature is particularly useful for quickly reviewing the content without needing to listen to the entire recording.

Additional Options: Within the recording note, users can also find options to share the audio, copy the transcript, or delete the recording if it is no longer needed.

This structured approach to storing and presenting call recordings and transcriptions enhances usability and ensures that important information is readily accessible.

Transcribing Calls

How Transcription Works

The call transcription feature in iOS 18.1 utilizes Apple Intelligence, the company's advanced artificial intelligence technology, to automatically convert the spoken words from a recorded call into text. The transcription process occurs in real-time during the recording, with the resulting transcript saved alongside the audio file in the Apple Notes app.

The transcription is divided into paragraphs, with each section labeled to indicate who is speaking. This formatting makes it easier to follow the flow of the conversation and attribute specific statements to the appropriate speaker.

Accessing and Reading Transcriptions

To access and read the transcriptions, follow these steps:

- Open the Notes app on your iPhone.
- Locate the "Call Recordings" section at the top of the app.
- Select the desired call recording to view its transcript.

The transcript will be displayed in a readable format, with paragraphs and speaker labels.

Use the playback controls at the bottom of the screen to listen to the recording while following along with the transcription.

Limitations of Transcription Accuracy

While the call transcription feature in iOS 18.1 is generally accurate, it is important to note that it may not be perfect. As an AI-based system, the transcription can sometimes misinterpret words or phrases, especially in cases of poor audio quality, heavy accents, or overlapping speech.

Users should treat the transcriptions as a helpful reference but not rely on them as a verbatim record of the conversation. It is always advisable to double-check critical information against the original audio recording.

Additionally, the transcription feature is currently limited to specific languages, including English, Spanish, French, German, Japanese, Mandarin Chinese, Cantonese, and Portuguese. Users who speak other languages may not have access to this functionality.

CHAPTER THREE

Using the Summary Feature

How to Generate a Summary of the Call

To generate a summary of a recorded call in iOS 18.1, follow these steps:

Access the Notes App: After completing your call, open the Notes app on your iPhone.

Locate the Call Recording: Navigate to the section labeled "Call Recording," where you will find your most recent recordings.

Select the Desired Recording: Tap on the recording you wish to summarize. This will open the transcript of the call.

Generate the Summary: At the top of the transcript, you will see a Summary button. Tap this button to allow Apple Intelligence to analyze the transcript and generate a concise overview of the call content.

Review the Summary: The summary will provide a brief outline of the main points discussed during the call, making it easier to grasp the essential information without reviewing the entire transcript.

Benefits of Using Summaries

Utilizing the summary feature offers several advantages:

Time Efficiency: Summaries condense lengthy conversations into key points, allowing users to quickly understand the main topics discussed without having to listen to the entire recording or read through the full transcript.

Improved Focus: By highlighting the essential elements of a call, summaries help users focus on critical information, which is particularly useful for busy professionals who need to manage multiple calls and meetings.

Enhanced Documentation: Summaries serve as an effective documentation tool, providing a quick reference for important discussions. This is beneficial for record-keeping in business contexts, ensuring that vital information is easily accessible.

Facilitated Review: Summaries can aid in the review process before follow-up actions or meetings, allowing users to refresh their memory about key points without delving into detailed transcripts.

Overall, the summary feature enhances the usability of the call recording and transcription capabilities in iOS 18.1, making it a valuable tool for both personal and professional communication.

Playback and Navigation

Playing Back Recordings

Playing back your recorded calls in iOS 18.1 is straightforward and user-friendly. Here's how to do it:

1. Open the Notes App: Launch the Notes app on your iPhone.
2. Access Call Recordings: Navigate to the "Call Recordings" section at the top of the app.
3. Select a Recording: Tap on the specific recording you want to listen to.
4. Playback Controls: At the bottom of the screen, you will see playback

controls, including play, pause, rewind, and fast forward.

Play: Tap the play button to start listening to the recording.

Pause: Tap the pause button to stop playback temporarily.

Rewind/Fast Forward: Use the rewind and fast forward buttons to navigate through the recording.

Navigating Through Transcriptions

The transcription feature allows you to easily navigate through the text while listening to the recording:

Scrolling: You can scroll through the transcript as the audio plays. The text will highlight in real-time, indicating which part of the conversation is currently playing.

Jumping to Specific Sections: If you want to jump to a specific part of the conversation, you can scroll through the transcript and tap on the section you want to hear. The playback will automatically jump to that point in the audio.

Highlighting and Jumping to Specific Sections

To enhance your experience while reviewing recordings and transcriptions, iOS 18.1 provides options for highlighting and jumping to specific sections:

Highlighting Text: While reading the transcription, you can tap and hold on a word or phrase to highlight it. This is useful for marking important points or sections that you may want to revisit later.

Jumping to Highlights: If you have highlighted specific sections of the transcript, you can easily navigate back to them during playback. Simply tap on the highlighted text, and the audio will jump to that part of the recording.

These playback and navigation features make it easier to manage your recorded calls and their transcriptions, allowing for a more efficient review process and ensuring that you can quickly find and reference important information.

CHAPTER FOUR

Legal Considerations

Understanding Call Recording Laws

While the introduction of call recording and transcription in iOS 18.1 is a significant feature, it is crucial to understand the legal implications and restrictions surrounding call recording. Laws regarding call recording vary widely across different countries, states, and jurisdictions. Some key points to consider:

Many states in the U.S. have "two-party consent" laws, which require the consent of all parties involved in a conversation before recording can take place. Failure to obtain consent can result in legal consequences.

In some countries, call recording is completely prohibited without explicit permission from all participants.

Even in jurisdictions where call recording is legal, it is essential to inform all parties that the conversation is being recorded. The iOS 18.1 feature includes an audible notification to ensure transparency.

Best Practices for Compliance

To ensure legal compliance when using the call recording feature in iOS 18.1, consider the following best practices:

Be aware of the laws in your specific location and obtain consent from all parties before recording, if required by law.

Always inform participants that the call is being recorded, either verbally or through the automated notification provided by iOS 18.1.

Avoid recording sensitive or confidential information without proper authorization, even if the recording is for personal use.

Store and handle recorded calls securely to protect the privacy of participants.

Consult with legal professionals if you have specific questions or concerns about the legality of call recording in your circumstances.

By understanding the legal landscape and adhering to best practices, users can leverage the call recording feature in iOS 18.1 while respecting the privacy rights of all parties involved.

Troubleshooting Common Issues

Common Problems and Solutions

As with any new feature, users may encounter some issues while using the call recording and transcription functionalities in iOS 18.1. Here are some common problems and their solutions:

Call Recording Not Starting:

Solution: Ensure that you are tapping the recording icon during an active call. If the icon does not appear, check if your device is running the iOS 18.1 developer beta and that you are using an iPhone 15 Pro or Pro Max.

Participants Not Hearing the Notification:

Solution: The notification stating "This call will be recorded" should be audible to all participants. If they do not hear it, try restarting your device or checking your volume settings.

Transcription Not Available:

Solution: After the call ends, wait a moment for the transcription to process. If it still does not appear, ensure that you have a stable internet connection, as the transcription may require online processing.

Audio Quality Issues:

Solution: If the recording sounds muffled or unclear, try to ensure that you are in a quiet environment during the call. Additionally, check that your microphone is functioning properly and not obstructed.

App Crashes or Bugs:

Solution: Since this feature is part of a beta release, occasional bugs may occur. Restart the Notes app or your device, and consider reporting the issue through Apple's feedback channels.

Tips for Improving Recording Quality

To ensure the best possible quality for your call recordings, consider the following tips:

Choose a Quiet Environment: Conduct calls in a quiet space to minimize background noise, which can interfere with audio clarity.

Use a Good Microphone: If possible, use a high-quality headset or external microphone to enhance audio input quality.

Check Signal Strength: Ensure you have a strong cellular or Wi-Fi signal during the call, as poor connectivity can affect both audio quality and the recording process.

Avoid Speakerphone Mode: If you are using speakerphone, consider switching to handheld mode to reduce echo and improve audio clarity.

Regularly Update Your Device: Keep your iPhone updated with the latest software versions, as updates may include improvements and bug fixes for the call recording feature.

By following these troubleshooting steps and quality improvement tips, users can enhance their experience with the call recording and transcription features in iOS 18.1.

Advanced Features

Future Updates and Features in iOS

With the release of iOS 18.1, Apple has introduced several advanced features, particularly focusing on AI capabilities under the umbrella of "Apple Intelligence." Future updates are expected to expand these functionalities significantly. Some anticipated features include:

Improved Siri: Enhancements to Siri's responsiveness and capabilities, allowing for more natural interactions and complex task management.

Summarization Tools: New tools for summarizing content across various applications, including emails and Keynote presentations, making it easier for users to digest information quickly.

Writing Tools: Features that assist with rewriting, proofreading, and summarizing text, enhancing productivity for users who frequently create written content.

AI-Powered Photo Editing: Advanced editing options that utilize AI to enhance images, including features like the Image Wand in the Notes app.

Priority Notifications: A system that prioritizes important notifications, ensuring users do not miss critical alerts.

These features are designed to leverage the processing power of the latest hardware, specifically the A17 Pro chip found in the iPhone 15 Pro and Pro Max, to deliver a seamless and intelligent user experience.

Integrating with Other Apps

The integration of Apple Intelligence with other applications is a key focus for enhancing user experience. Some notable integrations include:

Mail and Messages: The new summarization and smart reply features in Mail and Messages allow users to manage communications more efficiently. This integration helps users quickly respond to messages and understand email content without needing to read everything in detail.

Third-Party App Support: Apple is expected to extend its AI features to third-party applications, allowing for a broader range of functionalities, such as summarization tools and writing assistance in apps beyond Apple's ecosystem.

Cross-Platform Compatibility: Users can also expect integrations with Macs and iPads that support Apple Intelligence, enhancing continuity across devices. This means that features like AI-powered writing tools and photo editing can be utilized seamlessly on different Apple devices, providing a cohesive experience

As Apple continues to develop and refine its AI capabilities, users can look forward to more integrated features that enhance productivity and streamline everyday tasks across various applications.

Conclusion

Recap of Key Points

In this guidebook, we have explored the call recording and transcription features introduced in iOS 18.1, specifically for the iPhone 15 Pro and Pro Max models. Key points covered include:

Requirements for using the features, including device compatibility and installing the iOS 18.1 developer beta

Step-by-step instructions for recording calls and understanding the recording icon and notifications

Accessing and understanding the format of recorded calls and transcriptions in the Apple Notes app

How the transcription process works and the limitations of transcription accuracy

Playback and navigation options, including highlighting and jumping to specific sections

Legal considerations and best practices for ensuring compliance with call recording laws

Troubleshooting common issues and tips for improving recording quality

Future updates and integrations expected in iOS, leveraging Apple Intelligence across various applications

Encouragement to Explore Features

With the introduction of these advanced features in iOS 18.1, Apple has taken a significant step forward in enhancing user productivity and communication. By leveraging the power of AI and seamless integration across devices and applications, the call recording and transcription capabilities offer a valuable tool for professionals and personal users alike.

We encourage you to explore these features and integrate them into your daily workflow. Whether you are conducting important meetings, capturing interviews, or simply wanting to document conversations for future reference, the call recording and transcription functions in iOS 18.1 can streamline your processes and improve efficiency.

As Apple continues to refine and expand these features in future updates, users can look forward to an even more intelligent and integrated user experience. Stay tuned for further advancements and enjoy the benefits of this cutting-edge technology in your iPhone 15 Pro or Pro Max.

www.ingramcontent.com/pod-product-compliance
Lightning Source LLC
Chambersburg PA
CBHW072000210526
45479CB00003B/1011